A Handbook to the Art Of Wax-Flower Making

E. J. Jaques

ISBN 978-1-300-26458-3

WAX FLOWER
MAKING

A HANDBOOK

TO THE

ART OF WAX-FLOWER MAKING.

A HANDBOOK

TO THE

ART OF WAX-FLOWER MAKING.

BY

E. J. JAQUES,

ARTISTE IN WAX FLOWERS.

"Flowers have a soul in every leaf."—MOORE.

LONDON:

HOULSTON & WRIGHT, 65, PATERNOSTER ROW.

1862.

LONDON:
R. BURTON, PRINTER, 18, SOUTH MOLTON STREET, W.

CONTENTS.

PREFACE.

"Blessed be God for flowers,
For the bright, gentle, holy thoughts that breathe
From out their odorous beauty like a wreath
Of sunshine in life's hours."

Mrs. Tinsley.

Flowers are the fairest objects of Creation, and this would be a wilderness world indeed without them: they form the theme of the poet's sweetest strains, and on them painters have lavished all their skill. In many countries they are regarded with superstitious reverence, and—

"In Eastern lands they talk in flowers,
And they tell in a garland their loves and cares;
Each blossom that blooms in their garden bowers,
On its leaves a mystic language bears."

But flowers are tender things, and, with their sweet perfumes, soon fade away; cold winter comes and nips them up, but still we can preserve their image: this, to the lover of flowers, forms a pleasing task; and whilst the artist paints them on canvas with consummate skill, there is a way by which they may be more completely imitated, so that—

> "Nature herself might almost be deceived:"

viz., by modelling them in wax. To give instruction in this art, and in order that it may be more generally known, the following pages have been written; the want of a cheap and yet comprehensive treatise on the subject having been felt by many.

The art of modelling in wax is both an amusing and useful occupation. Many persons, however, think it very difficult to attain, which is not the case, and therefore do not direct their attention to it.

The writer has had much experience in the art, and trusts that while the book may prove invaluable to the beginner, many hints will also be found worthy the attention of the more experienced Artiste.

In the treatment of the subject throughout, the clearest and plainest definitions have been used, so as to be neither tedious in explanations, nor so compressed as not to be intelligible and practically useful.

E. J. J.

WAX-FLOWER MAKING.

MATERIALS REQUIRED.

The best materials in the end will prove the cheapest, because the flowers will look superior, last longer, and give the artiste greatest satisfaction.

WAX

Is obtained in packets containing twelve sheets, either single or double. It is prepared in the various colours required, viz. :—

White.
Green, in different shades.
Yellow, in different shades.
Pink.
Blue.

COLOURS.

These are procured in small bottles, varying in price according to the different colours, from 6d. to 1s. The following are required:—

Carmine.	Orange.
Vermilion.	Orange (dark).
Lake.	White.
Lemon.	Blue, in three shades.
Yellow.	

The following cake-colours are also required:— Lake; Smalt; Sepia.

BRUSHES.

Two kinds are used—Camel's-hair for veining, etc., and Hog's-hair for general use. The latter must never be dipped in water. The number required is as follows:—

Two fine camel's-hair.

Twelve hog's-hair (manufactured on purpose for this art).

WIRE.

Cotton and silk wires of various sizes, white and green; the white is used for delicate flowers.

MODELLING PINS.

Three china-headed pins, of different sizes, and one ivory-headed.

MISCELLANEOUS ARTICLES.

Small pair of embroidery scissors.

Palette, or saucers, for mixing colours.

Bottle of Down; this is used for the calyx of geraniums, hollyhocks, etc.

Bottle of Bloom, for rubbing the petals of certain white flowers.

Two pieces of marble, ¾-inch thick by 4 inches square.

A bottle of gum-water.

PATTERNS.

These may be purchased, but should the pupil be desirous of obtaining a correct copy of any flower, the following plan should be adopted:—Pick a natural flower in pieces, observing the number of petals of equal size. For instance, in a cabbage-rose there are five petals of one size, ten of another, and so on. It is only necessary to take one copy of each size, but to prevent mistakes, the number should be written on it. To obtain copies, lay the petal flat on a sheet of note-paper, placing the thumb of the left hand on the bottom and the forefinger at the top; take a large-sized brush with a moderate quantity of colour, and paint round the edge; remove the petal, and cut with scissors inside the colour.

MIXING COLOURS.

A small quantity should be taken from the bottle with the point of a penknife—to prevent waste—and laid on the palette; dip the point of the handle of a large hog's-hair brush in water, and let it *drop from* the handle on to the colour; hold the brush perpendicularly and rub round, friction adds to the brilliancy; the colour must not be mixed too thick, or, when dry, the flower would look rough and unfinished.

To obtain certain colours, it is necessary to mix them together, viz.:—The darkest shade of blue and middle shade of yellow, produces Green; lake and a small quantity of white for Pink; middle blue and lake, Purple. Brilliant Scarlet: Yellow wax, painted with carmine, for Scarlet Geranium; Deep Crimson: Carmine, and a very small portion of middle blue; rich brown for Wallflower, etc. Sepia and carmine: Mauve (for Lilac) lake, white, and middle blue.

PAINTING.

Place the wax petal on a piece of white paper, hold the bottom with the forefinger of the left hand, dip a brush in the colour, and pass it quickly and firmly over the petal, taking care to leave the bottom part free.

In painting variegated petals, it will be found convenient to turn them upside down, and in fine strokes, as in the Crocus, a small camel-hair pencil should be used, which must be moistened by the mouth.

BLOOM.

This is used for white flowers, to give them a velvet-like appearance. A small portion should be placed on the petal and rubbed with the finger, leaving the bottom free.

DOWN.

This must never be touched with the fingers, but shaken on the calyx, which is to be previously moistened with gum-water, and that which does not adhere, blown off.

GENERAL REMARKS.

The Pupil being furnished with the foregoing articles, will do well to observe, before commencing to model, the following hints:—

The artiste should not attempt to make or colour

any flower without having a natural one to look at; it will be advisable to obtain two flowers as nearly alike as possible, one to be taken to pieces, and the other to assist the artiste in its formation.

A difference will be observed in the surfaces of the sheets of wax, one side being rather glossy, and the other dull and slightly grained. In cutting out a flower, the pattern must always be placed on the dull side of the wax, and should never be cut across the grain.

For some flowers it is necessary the wax should be thicker than the ordinary sheets; to obtain this, press firmly the shining sides of two sheets together.

No water, colour, or grease, should be allowed to come near any portion of the wax which has to adhere to any part of the flower.

A sheet of paper should be laid on the table, on which must be placed the necessary articles for the flower intended to be produced.

A glass of warm water should be at hand, in which to dip the scissors and pins, as neither must ever be used without being moistened.

A seat should be chosen in a warm situation, and if the hands are too cold, they may be washed in warm water, and *must always* be kept clean.

Care should be taken never to lay the flower downwards on the table, and to prevent this, a wide-necked bottle should be provided in which to place it when requisite.

The following terms must necessarily be employed, an explanation of the same is therefore appended:—

Petals—the leaves, or principal part of the flower.

Pistil—that which protrudes farthest in the centre of the flowers, as in the Fuchsia.

Stigma—this is the top or thick part of the pistil.

Stamina—the filaments around the pistil, the tops of which are termed Anthers, or Apices.

Farina—the powder on the anther.

Calyx—the green at the back of the flower.

WHITE JESSAMINE.

This flower is selected as being one of the most simple for a beginner.

The petals, five in number, are cut from double white wax; the stamen, consisting of three filaments, cut from double lemon wax. These are *made by folding* the end of the sheet of wax three times about the twelfth part of an inch to form the Anthers. Rub the petals with bloom, being careful to leave the narrow part free; take a piece of rather fine wire about three inches in length, and prepare the stem by moulding a narrow strip of very light green wax smoothly round it; place the stamen round the top of the wire not too high; roll the middle-size pin firmly down the back of the broad part of the petal; press the front and narrow part with the stem of the pin; place the five petals at equal distances round the stamen, pressing them in their proper places, and bend the broad part of the petals back tinge the tube part of the flower slightly lemon, and, when dry, lay on a very little carmine. The calyx consists of five sprigs cut from double dark green wax; these are similar to the stamen, but without the anther, and placed round the bottom of the flower.

PYRUS JAPONICA.

Six petals of double yellow wax, all of the same size; these are coloured with carmine on both sides. The stamen is cut in one piece from double white wax, the anthers tipped with orange. To do this, hold the stamen between the thumb and finger of the left hand, and pass a brush moistened with orange colour along the tops of the anthers; take a piece, of middling-sized wire, bend the end down twice, about the third of an inch, over which mould a strip of light-green wax—(this in future directions will be called the foundation)—place the stamen round the foundation, pressing it with the fingers firmly at the bottom. To model the petals, hold the same in the palm of the left hand, and press in the centre of each with the forefinger; this gives a roundness to the petal, which should be most at the bottom; now take the smallest-sized modelling pin, and roll the head up the centre of each petal and then down each side, model the narrow part of the petal with the pin itself, fix three of the petals at equal distances round the stamen and the other three outside in the intermediate spaces; the calyx consists of six points cut in one piece from double dark-green wax; roll the head of the pin down each point, and two or three times across the bottom of the calyx; place round the base of the flower; the stem is covered with wax to match the calyx.

ORANGE BLOSSOMS (*Citrus*).

Cut from double white wax six petals; bloom them; stamen cut in double white wax, tinged orange; the foundation as in previous flower; place the stamen round the same; to model the petals, roll the head of the smallest pin down the centre of the back of the petal on the side which is not bloomed, press the pin down each side of the front, and roll the narrow part with the head of the pin on the same side; place the petals round the stamen as in the previous flower, turning the bloomed side towards the stamen, and bending the tops slightly back; calyx, a small piece of double light-green wax twisted round the bottom of the flower, and modelled smooth between the thumb and finger; stem, the same colour.

SCARLET GERANIUM.

Cut from double yellow wax five petals, three small and two large; paint on both sides with carmine; cut five short white filaments for stamen; place round a small foundation, and colour with carmine; model the petals by pressing the backs with the forefinger of the right hand; make a small crease, extending halfway up the petals, with the pin; affix the petals, the two largest uppermost, the three small ones under; calyx, five points of double light-green wax placed round the foundation, washed over with gum-water, and a little Down shaken over it.

CABBAGE ROSE (*Rosa Centifolia*).

Cut the petals from single white wax. Of course the number varies according to the size of the rose; an ordinary one consists of about fifty petals of different sizes, as nearly as follows:—

10	smallest size, which we will call		No. 1
10	next size,	ditto	2
10		ditto	3
5		ditto	4
15	largest size		5
—			
50			

Colour with lake mixed with a little flake white on both sides, tinting the five outer petals paler than the others; make the foundation of white wax cone-shaped, colouring the top with pink. To model the petals, press the thumb in the centre of each;

with the pin curl one edge of the petals Nos. 1, 2, and 3, forward, and the other back, varying the edges to prevent formality; No. 4 is to be deeply cupped, and the edges curled forward; size No. 5 deeply cupped, and the edges turned back: this is done by rolling the head of the pin at the back at the edges of the petals. To make up flower, place five of the petals size No. 1, round the foundation, turning them different ways; place the other five of the same size at the back of them; then five of No. 2 size, behind the last, and so on in rows of five to the end. The calyx consists of five points of double light green wax; roll the head of the pin firmly down the centre, and place these at the base of the flower; to make the seed-cup, or bottom part of the calyx, take a sheet of double light green wax, double it, then turn about half an inch down of the top to form a ridge, cut the necessary length required to roll round the bottom of the calyx, and neatly unite.

Buds are constructed the same as the flower; only, of course, the petals are smaller, and less in number. Also the calyx and seed-cup.

MOSS ROSE (*Rosa muscosa*).

This is made and coloured the same as the Cabbage Rose, only it consists of fewer petals; the calyx is cut out the same. Take a small fine spray of moss, press with a hot iron, warm the wax calyx before the fire, and press the moss with the help of the pin upon it. The cup is made the same as in the Cabbage Rose, and the moss pressed on as before, and coloured slightly with a brush moistened with carmine.

CHINA OR TEA-ROSE (*Rosa Safrano*).

The petals are cut from wax prepared by placing two sheets of single white wax and a lemon sheet between, which are to be pressed very firmly together. Colour slightly with lemon, and when dry very faintly tint with orange; afterwards, when this is dry, tint with crimson lake in cake. To model the petals, take the large ivory pin and cup very deeply, turning the edges of the first sets of petals forward with the pin, and the two last rows back with the head. Make the foundation large and cone-shaped, and colour the point the same as the flower. Place the petals round in rows of three, except the last row which consists of four. The calyx and seed-cup cut from double middle-green, and to be rather small; this and the backs of the outer petals are to be coloured with carmine.

WHITE ROSE (*Rosa alba*).

The petals are cut from single white wax, bloomed on both sides; the three smallest sets to be coloured towards the lower ends with lemon, and modelled or curled in the same manner as the Cabbage Rose. The stamina shows in this flower, which is made as follows:—Cut from double lemon forty filaments or threads, divided into clusters of eight; the anthers coloured with orange, and when dry a few here and there with brown (carmine and sepiá), these are placed in between the five smallest petals, turning in different directions. Place the petals on in sets of five, turning the last two rows back. Calyx and cup, light-green tinted with carmine.

YELLOW ROSE.

Cut the petals from lemon wax; colour them at the lower ends with orange, shading it off towards the upper end of each petal; place them on singly five in a row after the three first sets, which are placed on in clusters of five; the foundation as in previous roses, and the stamina shows from the front of the flower; calyx and cup as usual.

PINK MONTHLY ROSE.

Cut the petals from thin white wax, and colour pale-pink; mould them with the head of the large pin, to give a round appearance; make a small foundation of white wax, cone-shaped, on a middle-sized wire; place the three smallest petals round first to cover it; the remainder are placed on three in a row. Calyx as in other roses. Two or three green buds are a great improvement. Leaves very small.

CRIMSON ROSE (*Rosa Gallica*).

This flower is smaller than the Cabbage Rose, and constructed like the last one. The stamina cut from lemon wax tinted *only* with orange, and the petals coloured with carmine on both sides.

FUCHSIA.

Cut the four long or outside petals from double white wax, colour outside entirely with carmine, and inside halfway; the four inside petals are cut from single white wax and coloured purple; the stamina, consisting of eight filaments, is cut from double lemon and painted with carmine; the anthers, dipped in gum-water and then in lemon, mixed with white (powder); the pistil is cut from double white wax, about an inch and three-quarters in length, with the end turned down to form the stigma, painted purple, dipped in gum-water and then in the lemon and white powder used for the stamina. Fine wire for the stem, covered with light-green wax; press the pistil on the foundation, and pass the stamen round. To model the purple petals, roll the head of the largest pin down the centre and place round the stamen; to model the outside petals, roll the head of the pin on the inside at the lower end; model the part perfectly free from colour with the pin itself, place them outside the purple petals at equal distances, and neatly unite them by the aid of the pin; it will be requisite to recolour the tube part again. The calyx consists of a strip of double middle-green wax moulded neatly round the bottom of the flower.

WHITE FUCHSIA.

This flower is constructed the same as the last one, but coloured differently; the inner petals, stamina, and pistil, being coloured pink (lake and white); the outside petals bloomed and the exterior of the lower ends tipped with green. Stamina and pistil dipped in lemon and white, as in former flower.

FORGET-ME-NOT.

This flower is cut from double white wax in one piece; prepare the foundation by bending down the end of a fine wire and moulding round it a very small piece of white wax, pierce a hole in the centre of the flower, and pass the thin end of the wire through, leaving a small portion of the foundation visible, moulding it at the back with the point of the pin to fix it; make four little dents with the point of the pin in the part of the foundation to be seen, and colour the dents with yellow.

The flower must be painted after it is made with the lightest blue, mixed with a very small portion of middle-blue, round the edges, leaving the centre clear; the stem to be covered with light-green wax.

LABURNUM.

The petals, five in number, cut from single yellow wax; the largest dotted towards the middle, on the dull side, with brown. Make a small foundation of yellow wax, on fine wire, about an inch in length; mould the two smallest petals by rolling the head of the pin up the centre, place these on the foundation facing each other, forming a kind of bud; mould the next two as before, and place on in the same position, but not closed, bending them slightly forward; the petal, dotted brown, is placed at the back; the calyx consists of three points of green wax cut in one piece. To make a cluster, (of course the size chiefly depends on the taste of the artiste), take a piece of fine wire and cover with light-green wax; a few buds, formed by moulding with the fingers a piece of yellow wax at the end of the wire, to the shape required, give it a more graceful appearance. To arrange the flowers in their proper positions begin by placing three round the lower end after the buds, and so continue increasing the number towards the end of the stem; these are attached by firmly pressing the short stems of the flowers to the long wire, and arranging them so as not to give a stiff appearance. Of course the size of the cluster greatly depends on the taste of the artiste, but seventeen flowers form a pretty one.

SCARLET VERBENA.

This is cut in one piece of double white wax, as in Forget-Me-Not, (see page 19,) and made the same. Colour with carmine, leaving a very small centre white, and tipping the top of the foundation lemon; they are arranged from seven to twenty-four in a bunch. To arrange for drooping, take a piece of wire, covered with light-green wax, place the smallest flower at the end, pressing the stem on the main branch, affix two leaves opposite each other, increasing in size, and so on up the stem.

WHITE VERBENA.

Constructed the same as the last flower. Cut from double white wax, bloomed, and the centre coloured lemon.

PURPLE VERBENA.

Colour with purple (lake and blue), the centre coloured yellow. The calyx consists of five very small points of middle green.

PINK VERBENA.

Colour pink (lake mixed with white), the centre yellow.

RHODODENDRON (*Rhododendron ponticum*).

Cut the petals, five in number, in two pieces, one forming three petals and the other two, from double white wax; colour them on one side half-way with peach colour, (lake, blue, and white,) the one with three petals dot in the centre with sepia; this is done with a fine camel's-hair pencil.

The stamen, consisting of ten filaments, and the pistil are cut from double white wax, and coloured pink; the anthers coloured brown, and when dry to be dipped in gum-water, and afterwards in lemon and white powder; the stigma to be darkened with crimson lake, and to be dipped in lemon and white powder. To model, roll the head of the pin round the edges on the sides of the petals not coloured, press the pin down the centre of each petal on the coloured side. The foundation is small, and made of light-green wax; press the pistil on to the foundation, roll the stamina round, letting the pistil rise higher, place the petals opposite each other, and where united to be neatly moulded with the pin; towards the base of the flower slightly tinge with pink; there is no calyx; stem light green. Rhododendrons grow in clusters of seven or more.

PINK AZALEA.

This is rather smaller than the last flower. The petals are coloured pink, and in every other respect is constructed as in former flower.

WHITE AZALEA.

This flower is smaller than the Rhododendron, but constructed precisely the same. Cut the petals, five in number, from single white wax, and dotted in the centre of the piece cut in three, with very light-brown, and then bloomed. The pistil and stamen coloured brown, darker than the dots. The calyx five points of light-green wax; mount in clusters of three.

There is another variety, which is dotted pink, and the stamen and pistil dipped in lemon and white powders: in every other respect the same.

YELLOW AZALEA.

The petals of this flower are cut singly from two different shades of wax—orange and yellow. The centre petal dotted orange. The stamen and pistil are cut from double wax, the anthers coloured orange, and the stigma green. Roll the head of the pin round the edges of the petals, and press the pin down the centre of each; place the pistil on a middle-sized wire, covered with light-green wax; and the stamen round. The centre petal dotted orange is placed on next, and the two orange each side; the yellow ones opposite; to be neatly united with the pin, and mounted in clusters with very short stems.

GUM-CISTUS.

This flower somewhat resembles the White Geranium, and has a very delicate appearance; it consists of five petals cut in double white wax, and bloomed; paint towards the lower end of each petal a spot and a few streaks upward, composed of crimson and sepia; the stamina, consisting of a considerable number of filaments, is cut from a sheet of double lemon wax, with the end turned down for the anthers. To make up the flower, twist the stamina round a small foundation, allowing it to rise in the centre, forming a kind of cone; model the edges of the petals at the back, to give them rather a crumpled appearance; place them round the stamina at equal distances. When the flower is full-blown the petals fall quite back. The calyx consists of five points made from middle-green, and a few sprigs, of the same colour affixed round it. The flowers of Gum-Cistus grow in clusters of two and three.

WHITE LILY (*Lilium candidum*).

The petals, six in number, are cut from double white wax and bloomed on one side; three are of one size and three another; the stamina consists of six pieces of fine white wire, about two inches in length; cover the wire with white wax, and form the anthers by twisting the end of the wire and attaching a piece of orange wax to it, dip in gum-water and then in orange-coloured powder; the pistil is formed of middle-sized wire, about two inches and a half in length, covered with light-green wax, and thickened at the end to form the stigma. It will be observed that this flower has two ribs or ridges on each petal; to form this, roll the head of the smallest-sized pin firmly down the unbloomed side, then press the pin on each side of the ridges on the bloomed side to make them more decided; model the edges of the petals with the pin to give them a rather crumpled appearance, being careful not to tear them; place the stigma on the end of a piece of rather strong wire, and pass a strip of double light-green wax round them, to which attach the stamina; place the three largest petals on (the bloomed side towards the stamina, etc.) at equal distances apart, and the three smaller in the intermediate spaces. There is no calyx; stem light-green.

NEMOPHILA.

Cut from double white wax five petals. (This flower is not coloured until made.) Cut six fine filaments for the stamina from white wax, with the edges rolled to form the anthers; pass these round a small foundation. Turn back the broad part of the petals by rolling with the head of the pin on the shining side of the wax, press the pin firmly down the centre of each, place them round the foundation, and neatly unite; colour the anthers dark purple, and the edges of the petals with light-blue; the calyx consists of ten points of middle-green wax cut in one piece, five points at the top and five at the bottom; the latter are smaller, and turned up after the calyx is put on the flower with the end of the pin.

YELLOW DAHLIA.

Cut the petals from double wax; choose pretty delicate shade; of course the number depends on the size of the flower; an ordinary one consists of about ninety petals, as follows:—

10	smallest size, No.	1
20	„	2
10	„	3
20	„	4
30	largest size	5
90		

Vandyke two strips of double lemon wax about three-quarters of an inch in depth. The foundation is cone-shaped, and formed of lemon wax about an inch deep, and nearly the same in diameter. Press the head of the middle-sized pin into each point of the two strips, and pass the same round the foundation, bending them forward so as to cover it; roll the head of the pin up the centre of each petal, and fold the edges together at the bottom, bending the tops back; these are placed on ten in a row, beginning with size No. 1, each set in the intermediate spaces behind the other; the calyx consists of ten points, five of single light, and five of double dark-green wax,—the former to be placed at the back of the flower, and the latter round the stem.

WHITE DAHLIA.

Modelled and made up the same as the last flower, from double white wax, and bloomed; one of the strips forming the middle to be made of very light-green wax, and the other of white; the petals slightly tinted with lemon at the lower ends.

WHITE CAMELLIA.

Cut from single white wax the following number of petals for a flower of ordinary size:—

Smallest size, No.	1	 3
Next ditto	2	 3
Next ditto	3	 6
Next ditto	4	 3
Largest ditto	5.	..... 15 or 20.

Colour the petals—sizes Nos. 1, 2, and 3—at the lower ends lemon, and bloom on both sides; bloom the remainder of the petals on the dull side. To model, roll the head of the pin down the centre of the three petals, size No. 1, and place them round a small cone-shaped foundation made of white wax, press the pin down the centre of all the remaining petals, and turn the edges of those numbered 3, 4, and 5, back, without creasing them; place them on in order at the back, and in between each other, the largest in rows of five; cut the calyx from double lemon wax, three large and three small, these are to be cupped with the head of the pin, tinge with light-green, and, when dry, tint with carmine; place the three largest on first, and the smaller set outside.

SCARLET CAMELLIA.

Constructed the same as the last flower, painted with carmine on both sides, leaving small spots free from colour on some of the petals.

CARNATION (*Dianthus*).

Cut the petals from single white wax, colour the smallest very deeply with carmine (a little sepia may be used to deepen the colour), the outer petals are coloured carmine alone on both sides; it will be observed the natural petals have a jagged appearance at the edges; this is done with the finest-pointed pin; hold the petal between the thumb and forefinger of the left hand, and press the point of the pin all round the edges, model

D

them carelessly with the pin, place them on a small foundation of green wax, the smallest first. The best directions that can be given for putting together this flower, is for the artist to observe the different ways the petals turn in the natural one. The calyx consists of five points of double light-green, two points of lemon placed opposite each other outside the former, and three points of light-green cut separately placed in between the latter at the base of the flower; the leaves cut from double middle-green wax, and bloomed. Two or three of these flowers, placed in a small glass jug, have a very natural appearance.

CARNATIONS (Variegated).

The petals are cut from single white wax, and bloomed. The edges are coloured with deep pink; this is done with a fine camel-hair pencil; roll the head of the middle-sized pin halfway up each petal at the back, then press the pin down the centre, and on each side to give a crimped appearance. The smallest set are placed on first; affix all the petals but the largest in an upright position; the latter turn partly back. The calyx as before.

There is another variety, constructed in the same manner, which has the edges coloured purple.

WHITE PINK.

The petals are not so large nor so many in number as in the former flower. They are bloomed; colour very faintly at the lower end of the broad part of each petal with lemon; fringe the edges with the scissors; made the same as last flower. The calyx as before.

PASSION FLOWER (*Passiflora cœrulea*).

Cut three pieces of double white wax about an inch in length, and the sixth of an inch in width, at the top decreasing to a point; place these round the end of a piece of wire covered with light-green wax; affix, about half an inch underneath these, a strip of double light-green wax and mould smoothly round; the stamina is placed at the bottom of this, it is made of double light-green, and has a piece of wax—cut from pattern—affixed at the end by pressing them with the head of a pin, and are tipped with orange; make a small foundation at about half an inch from these, pass round this and bend forward a strip of white wax, fringed and coloured purple; place another strip round this, but do not bend it. The rays are made as follows:—Cut some strips of double white wax, place the marbles in warm water and roll the strips perfectly fine and round; if the marbles stick, moisten them again; place the rays on the ends of two strips of green wax about an inch deep, and cut them perfectly even; colour one-third purple, another blue, and leave the same distance free from colour in the centre; press them round, allowing the previously-coloured purple strip to be visible turn the rays back with the pin. Cut the petals, ten in number, from wax prepared by placing sheets of lemon, green, and white wax together, the lemon in the middle; press them firmly, model the petals by passing the head of the pin up and down them several times and also round the edges; these are to be deepened on the green side up the centre, with dark green paint: place the narrowest set of petals round underneath the rays, and the other five, in between. The calyx is made of double middle-green wax, cupped, and is placed at the back of the flower. Buds for the above are composed of ten petals of the same wax, coloured and modelled the same. In the latter, make a distinct mark by rolling the head of the pin down the centre of each petal. Place these round a foundation, cone-shaped—the narrowest first, and the other five between. The calyx as in the flower. Tendrils are made by preparing a fine wire as if for a stem, and twisting round and round a pin.

SINGLE PINK HYACINTH.

The petals, six in number, are cut from double white wax in one piece, and coloured pink. When this is dry, a stripe is laid on of a deeper shade down the centre on the inside of each petal. Roll the head of the pin down the petals and across the base, to give a round appearance; neatly unite with the aid of the pin. The stamen is cut from double white wax, the anthers coloured black with Indian ink, and dipped in lemon and white powder. These are affixed to a short stem of white wire about an inch in length, and then passed through the previously-prepared bloom. Model neatly at the base with the pin. A number of these flowers are affixed round a thick stem of very light lemonish-green wax, modelled on a strong white wire, thick at the bottom, and tapering towards the top. The leaves are now placed on round the bottom of the stem.

A bulb may be made of small, irregular pieces of lemon wax, pressed round the bottom of the stem, and then some dark, green pieces. Make the bulb quite circular, and paint a dark purplish colour.

This, placed in a Hyacinth Glass, has a very natural appearance.

WHITE LILAC.

The petals, four in number, are cut in one piece from double white wax, and made like Forget-me-not, the centre coloured lemon. Bloom the flower after it is made. The buds are moulded solid, and marked at the tops with the pin to give a more natural appearance. A fine white wire should be used for the stem. Calyx, a small strip of double light-green wax passed round the base of each. They are mounted on a separate stem covered with light-green wax, three and four in a cluster. Cut the stems of the flowers rather short. The buds are placed on first. Be careful *not* to place the flowers all on one side of the stem.

PEACH LILAC.

Made the same as white lilac, and coloured with lake, white and middle blue; it requires a little judgment as to the proportions. Centre painted lemon. Calyx as before.

CLEMATIS.

The petals, four in number, are cut from double white wax. Roll the pin over each, and press down the centre, with the small pin. Bloom them. Press a sheet of pale lemon and a sheet of light green wax together, and cut the stamen from it: pass round the end of a fine wire, and place the petals at equal distances round. Mount in clusters on a wire covered with green wax. The sprigs on the stem are placed on two and two, opposite each other.

WHITE WATER-LILY.

The petals are cut from double white wax, the four largest from two sheets of white and one of middle-green; a wire for the stamen or centre.

Cut about sixteen narrow strips from double orange wax, an inch and a half in length; tip them brown, the rest of the centre cut from pattern from double yellow wax. Take a piece of strong wire, and cover with light, green wax. Take a piece of double yellow wax, about half an inch in depth, and pass round the end of the wire to form a foundation about three-quarters of an inch in diameter. Indent with pin. Place the sixteen strips of orange wax at equal distances round the foundation. Place the yellow centre petals on ten in a row, and in between each other. Roll the head of the large pin up the sides and down the middle of each petal. The petals are placed on four in a row in between each other; the last four are to be shaded up the centre with brown on the green side. The last three rows of petals have a middle-sized white wire placed halfway up each to support them; this wire should be about three inches in length. Finish the stem of the flower by covering with light-green wax.

APPLE BLOSSOM.

The petals, five in number, are cut from double white wax; tinge the backs of some with rose colour. The stamen is cut from lemon and white wax pressed together about an inch in depth, and the ends turned down to form the anthers; colour several with orange. The pistil is cut from light-green wax, and placed at the end of a middle-sized wire, on a small foundation of green wax, and the stamen passed round. The petals are next affixed at equal distances; first being modelled with the middle-sized pin. Calyx five points of middle-green wax cut in one piece and placed at the back of the flower, and afterwards sprinkled with Down.

Buds are pinker than the flower, and calyx the same. They grow in clusters.

SNOWDROP.

The petals, six in number, are cut from double white wax; the three inner petals have a stripe and a spot near the end of each painted green with the sable brush; bloom; model the petals by rolling the head of the middle-sized pin down each. The stamina is cut from yellow wax, and placed round. The three uncoloured are placed on a small foundation of light-green wax, and the three with the spots in the intermediate spaces; a small piece of lemon wax is placed round where the flowers are united, tinged with brown.

CROCUS.

The petals, six in number, are cut from double orange wax; the three outer ones are striped with eight or ten pencil strokes of middle-green, broad at the end, and carried to a fine point. These strokes extend up about two-thirds of the flower. The stamen is cut from orange wax. Make a small foundation of white wax and place the stamen on. The petals are to be rolled with a large-sized pin down the centre and the edges, to give them a roundness; the three unstriped petals are placed on first, and the others in the intermediate spaces. The calyx, lemon-wax tinged brown.

WALLFLOWER.

Cut the petals, four in number, from double orange wax; they are painted with rich brown (sepia and carmine), and the centre of each petal is to be pressed with the finger, to give a creased appearance. The stamen is made from double lemon wax, and the anthers painted green. The calyx consists of four points, cut in one piece from middle green wax, and painted brown. The buds —some yellow and some brown—are made solid; a few half-open buds should be made: vary the flowers by making some light and some dark. The calyx for the buds is the same, only smaller.

MYRTLE.

Cut the petals from double white wax, and bloom and cup with the head of the middle-sized pin. Cut the stamen very fine from single white wax, and colour the edges pale-yellow, and pass round the end of a fine white wire; brush the stamen out nicely with the brush previously used for colouring them. Place the petals round, and paint the backs of some of them rose-colour. The calyx consists of five points cut in one piece from green wax; the buds are moulded solid from lemon wax, and tinged slightly with red. Calyx as in the flower; the leaves must be rubbed with the hand to give a glossy appearance. Mount the leaves first, buds next, and then the flowers.

FOLIAGE.

This branch of the art is very often neglected; much of the beauty of a group of flowers is lost by the ill-arrangement of the leaves. They can, of course, be purchased, but the artiste may think it worth while to make them. The following directions apply to nearly all kinds of leaves.

A common Rose-leaf is selected for example. Procure a perfect leaf. Take two sheets of light-green wax, press them firmly together; take a small piece of middling-sized wire, place it on the wax to form the stem; take a sheet of darker green, the colour of the leaf, and overlay the two sheets and wire, and press them together. Cut, with the dull side uppermost, a rough form of the leaf; dip the wax one, in warm water, and press it quickly on the natural leaf; cut it to the proper shape while on the real leaf. Tinge the edges with carmine, and mount in threes.

GROUPING.

Of course the appearance of a group of flowers is greatly enhanced by a careful selection and proper arrangement in the blending and harmonizing of the colours together. The refined taste easily perceives when this is not the case; as discord in music grates on the musician's ear, so the slightest violation of a proper arrangement of colours is painful to the eye:—

> "Nature herself delights to see
> Her various works in unity."

The following hints may prove acceptable to the inexperienced artiste:—

A pretty group for a vase may be composed of the following flowers:—Scarlet Camellia, White and Yellow Jessamine, Nemophilla, Laburnum, Verbena. Another vase to correspond: — White Camellia, Pyrus Japonica, Yellow Jessamine, Nemophilla, Passion Flower, and Fuchsia. Another group may be composed of different-coloured Roses, also of various shades of Carnations, or of Wallflowers, placed in a small glass jug. An elegant group is formed of entirely drooping flowers, such as Westeria, Laburnum, or all Passion-flowers, or various-coloured Fuchsias. Dahlias, Geraniums, and White Jessamine, in groups, look very elegant, and this mode is not so common as that of arranging various flowers together which grow at different seasons, and which often destroys the natural effect.

IMITATION CORAL BASKETS.

These form very elegant and delicate receptacles for the flowers, and are both inexpensive and easily made. The frame is constructed with ordinary bonnet wire (white). A circle is made, and then the wire twisted so as to form about seven loops round it; next make a row of eight larger loops, and so on, increasing the size according to taste. Flatten the bottom of the basket, and bend the top loops up. Tie some pieces of thick knitting cotton in an irregular manner on the basket, in and out the loops. The wax can be procured at any oilshop or chemist's. It must be melted in a basin in the oven, and when in a liquid state, poured over the basket with a teaspoon. This is to be repeated until the wire is rather thickly covered.

A white wax basket may be filled as follows:—Rhododendron, orange-blossom, cabbage-rose, nemophilla, scarlet geranium, tea-rose buds, cineraria, white rose, wallflower, yellow azalea.

A BRIDAL BOUQUET.

A white rose for the centre; myrtle, orange-blossom, and white jessamine arranged in clusters round. A lace paper should be placed at the back, and the stems concealed either by a bouquet-holder or white satin ribbon twisted round.

In arranging a group for a vase, place the drooping flowers in first, then some moss. The other flowers should be arranged on one stem and then placed in the vase, and afterwards a little more moss.

To Imitate Red Coral.—The white wax must, when in a liquid state, be mixed with vermilion; about an ounce of the latter to half a pound of wax. The vermilion costs sixpence an ounce, the wax about three shillings per pound.

FINIS.

E. BURTON, PRINTER, 18, SOUTH MOLTON STREET, W.